Public Transportation

LET'S RIDE THE
CITY BUS!

Elisa Peters

PowerKiDS press™

New York

Published in 2015 by The Rosen Publishing Group, Inc.
29 East 21st Street, New York, NY 10010

First Edition

Editor: Amelie von Zumbusch
Photo Research: Katie Stryker
Book Design: Andrew Povolny

Photo Credits: Cover Richard Cummins/Lonely Planet Images/Getty Images; p. 5 Fedrico Rostagno/Shutterstock.com; p. 6 Photofusion/Contributor/Universal Images Group/Getty Images; p. 9 Matthew Gonzalez/E+/Getty Images; p. 10 iStock/Thinkstock; p. 13 Carmakoma/Shutterstock.com; p. 14 Science & Society Picture Library/Contributor/SSPL/Getty Images; p. 17 Miker/Shutterstock.com; p. 18 Chris Jenner/Shutterstock.com; p. 21 Tadeusz Lbrom/Shutterstock.com; p. 22 Stanislav Tiplyashin/Shutterstock.com.

Publisher Cataloging Data

Peters, Elisa.
Let's ride the city bus! / by Elisa Peters — first edition.
 p. cm. — (Public transportation)
Includes index.
ISBN 978-1-4777-6482-4 (library binding) — ISBN 978-1-4777-6483-1 (pbk.) —
ISBN 978-1-4777-6485-5 (6-pack)
1. Buses — Juvenile literature. I. Peters, Elisa. II. Title.
TL232.P4818 2015
629.28—d23

Manufactured in the United States of America

CPSIA Compliance Information: Batch #WS14PK4: For Further Information contact Rosen Publishing, New York, New York at 1-800-237-9932

CONTENTS

Have you ever taken a city bus? "Bus" is short for "omnibus."

5

Wait at the bus stop. When the bus comes, get on.

Make sure to get on the right bus! A **panel** on the front lists the route.

You pay a fare to ride. You can often pay with a **transit pass**.

Press the button or tape to tell the driver you want to get off at the next stop.

14

Horses drew the first buses. Next came steam-powered buses in the 1830s.

Today most buses run on gas. Hybrid buses are used, too. They pollute less.

17

15 St Paul's Cathedral Fleet Street Aldwych

TRAFALGAR SQUARE

15

RM1941

TURN TO OPEN

Buses with two levels are double-decker buses.

Articulated buses are extra long. Their two parts meet at a joint. This lets them bend.

21

Riding the bus is fun! It is an easy way to get around your city or town.

WORDS TO KNOW

articulated bus

panel

transit pass

WEBSITES

Due to the changing nature of Internet links, PowerKids Press has developed an online list of websites related to the subject of this book. This site is updated regularly. Please use this link to access the list: www.powerkidslinks.com/putr/cbus/

INDEX